Simple, straight-forward principles to help businesses be more PROFITABLE!

IN THE
BLACK

NINE PRINCIPLES TO MAKE YOUR BUSINESS PROFITABLE

This book is written for **business owners, operators** and **managers**. No matter what your position in your business, no matter what your product or service, and irrespective of your talent, skill, or experience, the principles presented in this book can make your business **more profitable!**

Every **chapter** is **filled** with **principles** and **concepts** that you can use **immediately** to become more profitable in your business and to enhance your expertise—and wisdom—in business decision-making.

IN THE
BLACK

To my
friend,
Ashish

3/27/19

IN THE
BLACK

NINE PRINCIPLES TO MAKE YOUR BUSINESS PROFITABLE

Updated Edition

ALLEN B. BOSTROM, CPA

Universal Accounting Center
5288 South Commerce Drive
Salt Lake City, Utah
84107

Published by
Universal Accounting Center
5288 South Commerce Drive
Salt Lake City, Utah 84107
areyouintheblack.com

All Rights Reserved. Except as permitted under the United States Copyright Act of 1976, no part of this book may be reproduced, translated, or electronically stored, posted or transmitted, or used with any format or medium whatsoever without prior written permission of the Publisher. This publication is sold with the understanding that neither the author nor the publisher is engaged in rendering legal, investment, accounting, or other professional services.

Books are available for business or quantity discounts.
Telephone the publisher at 800.343.4827.

Copyright © 2008 by Allen B. Bostrom, CPA

Printed in the United States of America

ISBN 978-0-9764702-2-9

C O N T E N T S

C O N T E N T S

continued

Acknowledgments

I have wanted to write this book for a long time. It has only been with the help of family members, business associates, and friends that the book has been completed and now updated.

This updated edition enhances the concepts presented in the initial version and makes application easier through better summaries and worksheets at the end of each chapter.

I extend a special thanks to:

- My wonderful wife Sheri for her love and support.
- Customers and clients for contributing input, feedback, ideas and stories for this book.
- My Universal Accounting Center associates for their dedication to excellence in marketing, production and accounting and for their valuable contributions to this book.
- And my father, Alf, a great businessman and dedicated father who made all of this possible through his great wisdom and special knack for teaching business concepts to people in the classroom and on the job. I am proud to be his son.

Thank you one and all.

Be sure to read the preview of my new book, *Red to Black in 30 Days*, which is at the end of this book. This new book is available now from Universal Accounting Center and major book retailers.

Foreword

What Arnold Palmer was to golf, my father, Alf Bostrom, was to small business! Although certainly not as well known, my father perfected the art and science of running profitable businesses. During his career, he managed 22 different businesses—up to eight at one time. Most were close to financial ruin when he took over, yet all became profitable and successful.

He operated those businesses by adhering to a set of principles that, when implemented, can transform any business. They were first proven in a variety of businesses: new and used car dealerships, clothing, appliance, furniture, and bakery goods stores and manufacturing ventures.

Many of the concepts in this book originated with my father. Since that time, I have tested, refined and added to these principles to make them more timely and universal in today's competitive environment. I feel confident that they can help you become more successful in your career or business when you apply them yourself.

A BRIEF HISTORY

As a young man, my grandfather Peter Lauritz Bostrom immigrated to Salt Lake City, Utah from

Sweden with nothing but a few dollars in his pocket and a desire for adventure. He endured the years of the Great Depression surprisingly well. Two things kept him employed: a reputation for hard work and integrity.

His son Alf maintained that legacy, and added strong managerial wisdom to it. Born in 1926, he was too young to remember the most severe parts of the depression, but he did learn the value of hard work. He developed a number of money-making ventures including wading through the water at the local golf course to collect golf balls which he would then sell to the weekend golfers.

When Alf was 16 years old, his father was killed in an automobile accident, so he had to take over part of the role of providing for his family. At 18, he joined the navy and fought in the Pacific Theater during World War II. He was in Tokyo Bay when the Japanese signed the peace treaty.

Upon returning to Utah, he met my mother, Betty Gene Blomquist, married, and started a family. He had a variety of jobs with small businesses, each being different and teaching him a new aspect of business. He identified certain universal principles that made businesses profitable and successful.

In the 1960's, Alf decided to venture out into business for himself and started a management company. For a percentage of the potential future profits, he would take over management of businesses that were experiencing huge losses, many on the brink of bankruptcy, and promise to turn them around. What business owner wouldn't take that offer? Alf didn't earn a dime unless the business became successful. These business owners had nothing to lose.

That's how my father earned the title of "The Turnaround King". Not only was he able to turn nearly every business that he managed around, but most are still in business today, several decades later.

Why do I provide so much history on my father? For two reasons:

1. He has lived an exemplary life and deserves recognition.

And,

2. I inherited that same passion for business. I watched him, learned from him, and enjoyed how much business owners respected his sound business advice. His example acted as a spring board for me as I have been able to learn from him and experience even more. I will always be grateful to him!

THE VALUE OF THIS BOOK

I wish I could play golf like Arnold Palmer. I can't. But I can manage businesses profitably, and teach you to do the same! You can gain this same expertise and use it in your own business endeavors.

I have found that there are three ways to evaluate a book like this:

1. I try to mentally apply some of the useful principles.

2. I find it powerful enough to apply the principles, and recommend the book to other people.

3. I am impressed enough to buy it for other people in the organization. And I expect them to read it, discuss the principles together as a group, and then decide how the principles can be applied in our particular setting.

This is what I would like you to do with this book in your organization.

I hope that you will recognize this book as a tremendous value and enjoy reading it as much as I enjoyed writing it.

1

Your Business Dream Can Become a Reality!

This book is written to **business owners, operators** and **managers.** No matter what your position in your business, or your product or service, and irrespective of your talent, skill, or experience, the principles presented in this book can make your business **more profitable!**

As a teenager, I remember accompanying my father on visits to many of the businesses he managed. The travel time would sometimes be over an hour and we would almost always discuss some aspect of the business we were visiting. He taught me "business" in terms that I could understand. For example: **"Nothing happens until you make a sale!"** This and other important principles often came up in our discussions. I have expanded and refined these into the **Nine Principles to make your business profitable** that will be presented in the following chapters.

An assessment of business practices usually leads to recommendations for specific changes: Some things can be changed immediately. Some recommendations will improve the business in the near future, and some will require a longer time to prove beneficial. In the following chapters, you will also learn how to make an accurate assessment of your own problem areas, then make plans for implementing profitable and properly-timed changes in your business.

Early in my career, I started helping friends with their entrepreneurial concerns. Like most small business owners, they were well-versed in marketing and production, but accounting and general business management were mysteries. Good business advice was critical to the financial health of their businesses. These friends were eager to implement these principles, when they were explained in a way that made sense.

These Nine Principles worked for them, and they can work for you, too!

Now a little bit about the framework of this book: You will learn about the **Universal Business Model** that focuses on how these principles work together in the three primary functions of business: **Marketing, Production and Accounting.** As with a three-legged stool, all three major functions are important, and attention must be given to all three to allow your business to grow. Ignoring any of the three may work for a short time, but eventually your business will suffer and perhaps fail.

The last chapter presents an **Improvement Process** that you can use to implement these principles. At the end of every chapter is a quick review of that chapter's major concepts with application suggestions and a place for notes.

Many books have been written on improving sales, production and business operations. This book will address those themes, and will put more emphasis on the third critical function of business—**Accounting.** When analyzed with knowledge and wisdom, the information from the accounting system will aid in making profitable business decisions in both Marketing and in Production.

Accounting is the language of business. But don't worry; you **don't need to be an accountant** to understand these concepts and principles. This book will help you understand how to make all three critical functions of your business **work together effectively!** You can then say: **"Now I get it!** I finally understand why accounting is so important because it helps me in every aspect of my business." **Then, your business dream can become a reality!**

Certain assumptions about making change can be made about small business people:

♦ They never have enough time.

♦ They never have enough money.

♦ There is always more to do.

When you finish each chapter, your work is not done. Nothing will change in your business until you commit to do something and then get busy. These principles are great but mean nothing unless you convert them into action.

At the end of each chapter are two important pages: The first is a **Chapter Review** which summarizes critical concepts from the chapter. The second is an **Action Planning** page which asks pertinent questions about application of those principles and provides space for planning action steps. This book can become your guidebook for change in the next few months and Action Planning section can make the principles and concepts from each chapter come alive in your business.

Take a few moments right now and complete your Chapter One Action Planning on Page 6

CHAPTER ONE REVIEW

Critical concepts to remember...

- The three major functions of business are Marketing, Production, and Accounting.

- You don't need to be an accountant to understand these Marketing, Production, and Accounting principles.

- Accounting is the guiding language for your business! Your accounting system should give you the critical information you need to help make necessary decisions concerning all aspects of your business.

Notes...

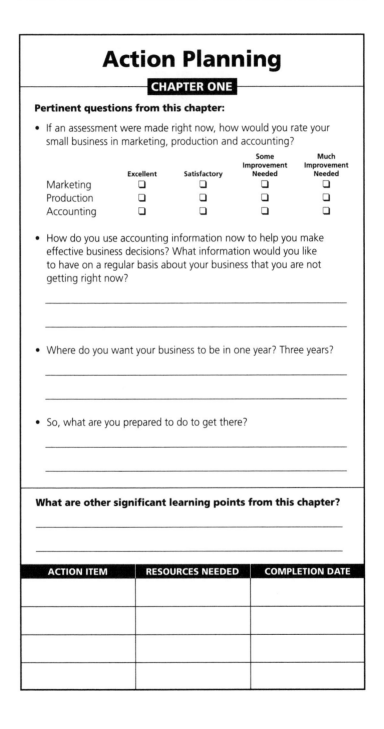

Action Planning

CHAPTER ONE

Pertinent questions from this chapter:

- If an assessment were made right now, how would you rate your small business in marketing, production and accounting?

	Excellent	Satisfactory	Some Improvement Needed	Much Improvement Needed
Marketing	❏	❏	❏	❏
Production	❏	❏	❏	❏
Accounting	❏	❏	❏	❏

- How do you use accounting information now to help you make effective business decisions? What information would you like to have on a regular basis about your business that you are not getting right now?

  _____

  _____

- Where do you want your business to be in one year? Three years?

  _____

  _____

- So, what are you prepared to do to get there?

  _____

  _____

What are other significant learning points from this chapter?

_____

_____

ACTION ITEM	RESOURCES NEEDED	COMPLETION DATE

Nine Principles to Make Your Business Profitable

I have always had a passion for business. I enjoy working with company owners and managers in improving their businesses, but I am often astonished at how little they know about their own companies.

In consulting with business owners, my initial analysis is always the same. I look critically at the three major functions of business—**Marketing, Production,** and **Accounting:**

- **Marketing** is the function of business that brings customers to your door and culminates in some sort of sale.

- **Production** is the function of business that deals with customers from the time of the first sale through the entire life of the relationship.

- **Accounting** is the function of business that gathers data and information from all the different aspects of the business.

I analyze how each of these functions is working separately. **More importantly,** I then evaluate how they work together.

I have created a simple model which defines my understanding of how to look at businesses objectively. I refer to it as the **Universal Business Model** which is illustrated below in its three different phases.

The first phase illustrates the three functions operating independently with little regard for what is happening in the other two functions. The functions could be running well independently, but with little synergy. The center core, where all circles intersect, represents total company profit. In accounting jargon, a profitable company is **IN THE BLACK**. Profit in the Phase I example is very small.

UNIVERSAL BUSINESS MODEL—PHASE I

Here are some examples of what Phase I looks like. The overlapping of the different circles indicates that little interaction occurs among the different functions:

- ◆ Marketing and Sales are occurring, but no one tells

Production of big new contracts that have just been signed where customization is involved.

◆ Production might be rolling along with no idea what costs are associated with producing certain final products. Or, the wrong products might be produced compared to which products are selling.

◆ The accountants seem to be tied to their desks, and never visit either the production floor or visit a potential customer with a sales person.

◆ Within the separate functions, everything seems to be going well, except for the complaints about the other departments.

In Phase II of the **Universal Business Model,** synergy begins to occur. Some communication takes place among the three functions, and it helps. It is certainly better than Phase I. The middle area **IN THE BLACK** indicates the potential profit for the business. In this case, profit is small—smaller than it should be, but certainly bigger than it was in Phase I.

UNIVERSAL BUSINESS MODEL—PHASE II

In Phase III of the **Universal Business Model,** illustrated below, the three major functions are working together well, and the goal is to maximize the area in the center core which represents profit. It is impossible to maximize profit without the three functions interacting well with each other. Here, profit is much bigger than it was in either Phase I or Phase II. The **Nine Principles** described in this book fit within these three functions and, when implemented effectively, will make the center core (profit) bigger.

UNIVERSAL BUSINESS MODEL
Phase III—When everything is working together

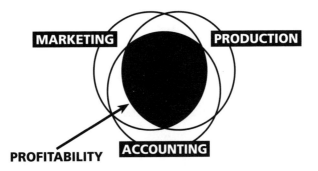

This illustrates the evolution from Phase I to Phase III. In our example case, Marketing works with Production to make sure the right products and services are ready at the right time. Accounting provides critical information to both Marketing and Production to help in making profitable decisions.

KEY OBSERVATIONS ABOUT THE UNIVERSAL BUSINESS MODEL

My first observation is that most businesses do **very well** in one of the functions, **partially** well in another, and **not well at all** in the third. **Accounting** is most often the one function that falls to the bottom of the list. This means that without proper guidance, many unprofitable decisions could be made.

Michael Gerber, in his book *The E Myth* (Harper Collins Publishers, 1988), described new businesses as having been started by a technician who had an "entrepreneurial seizure." They understood the technical side of the business, but were weak in Accounting. They may have learned early that Marketing and Production were vital, but were slow to add Accounting. Accounting is usually a BIG problem, especially for new or small businesses.

The **emphasis** of this book is on making all three major functions work together, focused on business goals. A secondary emphasis will be on using the **accounting function to provide the information** that the business owner or operational manager needs in order to see the whole picture of what is happening in his company or department, whether good or bad.

Sometimes these separate functions work well alone, but seem to have problems working together. Maybe you have been in this situation: Sales are great, but production is working on "overload," and customers aren't paying for their purchases. Sometimes you don't even know if you are making a profit! It is quite a dilemma. Increased sales are not always the answer, but they certainly help. Margins need to be in line, and expenses need to be under control.

One client had started a framing business prior to coming to Universal Accounting Center for assistance. He claimed that his sales were going through the roof, as he was successful in taking business from his competition on nearly every bid. (Perhaps this should have been the first clue that something was wrong.) With further analysis, we were able to show that he was selling the finished product for less than his cost. He had to bring all three major functions into sync before his business became profitable again.

Imagine if Accounting didn't step in with the proper information, his business could have plunged him into bankruptcy, even with high sales!

The major lesson is that the closer these three essential functions work together, the greater the profit. The ideal model would have all three circles on top of each other, working harmoniously **IN THE BLACK**. The ideal may not be totally possible, so the goal is to **make** the **center core,** where all three circles intersect, **as big as possible.** The focus of the **Universal Business Model** is to have open lines of regular communication between each of the three functions.

Another observation is that information from Accounting is critical to the success of the other two. This is the reason why implementing an accurate accounting system should be a first priority.

This leads to the following important concept: The **accounting system and the people who run it are tremendous assets** within a business. The accounting function is powerful in helping any business operator and department manager understand what is happening within the business.

The **Universal Business Model** has meaning in every phase of the business:

In **start-up businesses:** All three functions of the model have importance, with Accounting being the one aspect that keeps track of all start-up costs. This is extremely important when funds used for development purposes are borrowed, or if the decision is made to go public. Additionally, most businesses start with extremely limited resources, particularly capital. Attention must be diligently applied watching cash flow—both how much is coming in and how much is going out.

In **on-going businesses:** Whether profitable or not, the model allows you to focus your attention where it is most needed. Again, Accounting provides vital information to help the business owner or department manager make effective decisions, and ascertain his or her position in relation to competitors through "Benchmarking." (Discussed in Chapter Five).

In **turn-around businesses:** The **Universal Business Model** provides a great framework for analysis and development of plans that will help the business survive and become profitable. The information from the accounting system can usually pinpoint problems that need to be corrected right now, in the near future, and over the long-term. If you are working with a financial institution, accounting information is vital for you and the financial institution, to ensure that the partnership is working favorably for both you and them.

NINE PRINCIPLES TO MAKE YOUR BUSINESS PROFITABLE

With the Universal Business Model understood as a realistic view of your business, the nine management principles can now be introduced. Three principles are in each of the different functions of the model.

Effective management principles are the same everywhere, every time. Critical information used in necessary leadership decisions is the same in every case. The key is receiving this information in a consistent and timely manner.

Here are the **Nine Principles** that will be discussed in the remainder of this book. They are individually discussed in Chapters Three, Four, and Five. These chapters follow the Universal Business Model—Marketing, Production and Accounting, respectively.

MARKETING

Great customers don't just appear; they are made!

Principle 1— Nothing happens until you make a sale!

Principle 2— A deal is only good when it is good for **both** parties.

Principle 3— Grow your business geometrically.

See Chapter Three for more details on these principles.

PRODUCTION

Becoming the Expert on what happens inside the business.

Principle 4— Pour on the communication.

Principle 5— Improve your internal processes.

Principle 6— Take what you have and make it better.

See Chapter Four for more details on these principles.

ACCOUNTING

In The Black—Profit is the Answer!

Principle 7— Cash flow! Cash flow! Cash flow!

Principle 8— Know your business.

Principle 9— Plan for tomorrow.

See Chapter Five for more details on these principles.

As a bachelor, in my younger years, I learned how to make a sugar cake. It was a little treat that my roommate and I would enjoy at the end of the day. While living in Europe, I wasn't sure what temperature to use in Fahrenheit, so I guessed without doing the conversion calculation. I should have done that calculation since I apparently had the temperature too high.

I pulled the cake out when the top looked brown, but much earlier than I should have. Suspicious of the quick baking time, I cut into the cake and found the center to still be liquid. Not knowing better, I thought I would just re-stir it, lower the temperature and re-cook it; that seemed logical. It came out as a solid, five-pound, barbell weight. Following the recipe can bring success— departing from it brings far less-favorable results.

The action planning section at the end of this and each chapter will allow you to put in concrete terms what can be done in your own business to implement these principles and concepts.

Reading the book isn't enough! Action is required to change and improve all functions of your business.

Of course, I don't want to oversimplify this by suggesting that these principles will serve every business with a simple tweak. It is never that easy. Appropriate application of each principle is critical. There is no question that we all become better with experience and, from that experience, we learn wisdom which makes future application more effective.

THE WISDOM PYRAMID

The Universal Business Model illustrates a realistic approach to understanding your overall business. The **Nine Principles** outlined within the Universal Business Model work in any phase of a business. However, you don't become experts overnight in implementing these principles.

You hear a lot about the importance of making decisions based on **data.** What I have learned is that decisions should be based on **wisdom,** not necessarily data alone.

Admittedly, the better the data are that enter into the Wisdom Pyramid at the bottom, the better the information and knowledge will be that are developed along the way. Wisdom can be developed more quickly when the data are accurate and timely.

The **Wisdom Pyramid Model** below shows how you develop wisdom in our decision-making. This model **complements** the Universal Business Model extremely well in showing the **process** of learning, and becoming more effective in implementation. It also helps us understand that it takes time to become experts in using the **Nine Principles** to our advantage.

The Wisdom Pyramid (Source is W. Edwards Deming, in some of his quality work done after World War II. Other quality consultants have used similar models to illustrate how people learn.)

WISDOM

KNOWLEDGE

INFORMATION

DATA

Here are some helpful definitions:

Data—Numerical explanations of activities.

Information—Assembly of data into a usable, quantitative or qualitative form, probably some sort of report.

Knowledge—Interpretation and analysis of the information, and application of the information in realistic settings.

Wisdom—Intuition based on experience from applying information. (You almost know the outcome before you see the numbers.)

Now for the application:

Data is input into the accounting system. This data is accumulated and compiled within the system and, subsequently, becomes information. Because business decisions are made based on this information, it is important that the information be accurate and timely.

From that information, decisions are made, and knowledge and experience are gained. Over time and with practice, wisdom is developed. At this point, you can make decisions based on wisdom—not just on the data and information that are available. **You become the expert!**

In Chapter Five, you will learn that the data and the information in the Wisdom Pyramid usually come directly from the accounting system. The critical factor is that the accounting system of the business provides appropriate and accurate information that you need to eventually develop knowledge and wisdom.

Here is an example of how I have gained wisdom about what causes business failures. For years, I have worked with businesses of all sizes. Many were failing; some didn't make it. I was able to observe various reasons for these failures.

First, those observations were just data points. Then they became information, then knowledge, and then wisdom. The list below outlines the major reasons for business failures. As you can see, not all of these reasons can be learned from data and information. Rather, most of the reasons can be learned from the knowledge and wisdom developed through the years. In most cases, it started with accurate information gathered from the accounting system.

The Biggest Reasons for Business Failures

- ◆ Insufficient working capital (current assets less current liabilities)

- ◆ Inexperience

- ◆ Extravagance (spending money for unnecessary purchases)

- ◆ Dishonesty

- ◆ Overly optimistic or unrealistic outlook

- ◆ Personality issues

◆ Credit policies

◆ Incomplete accounting system

◆ Misunderstood accounting information

This list represents wisdom accumulated over the years which is critical in creating profitability. The **Wisdom Pyramid** provides a process for learning which is valuable in making better decisions which, in turn, will make your business more successful.

PUTTING THESE PRINCIPLES TOGETHER

In concept, these principles sound great. But application is the key! Specific steps are outlined in Chapter Six to help you implement these principles in your business. Issues of what to do immediately, in the near-term, and longer-term are addressed.

CHAPTER TWO REVIEW

Critical concepts to remember...

♦ The **Universal Business Model** will help you look at your business realistically and assign stewardships.

♦ The **Nine Principles** to Make Your Business Profitable fit within the **Universal Business Model** to help in its understanding and implementation.

♦ The **Wisdom Pyramid** is used as a learning model. Knowledge and wisdom are developed from data and information provided from the accounting process.

♦ Wisdom can be gained over time, with the implementation of the **Nine Principles.**

Notes...

_____

_____

_____

_____

_____

_____

_____

_____

_____

_____

_____

Action Planning

Pertinent questions from this chapter:

- What strengths and weaknesses exist in each of your three major business functions—Marketing, Production and Accounting?

	Strengths	Areas of Improvement
Marketing		
Production		
Accounting		

- Where are you in the Wisdom Pyramid in each of the three functions in the Universal Business Model?

	Data	Information	Knowledge	Wisdom
Marketing	❑	❑	❑	❑
Production	❑	❑	❑	❑
Accounting	❑	❑	❑	❑

- On what kind of information, knowledge, or wisdom do you base your business decisions?

_____

_____

What are other significant learning points from this chapter?

_____

_____

ACTION ITEM	RESOURCES NEEDED	COMPLETION DATE

Marketing

Great customers do not just appear; they are made!

When I was young, I remember going to work with my father and watching what he did. With few exceptions, he would first seek out the sales manager and start asking questions. "How are sales going? What are customers buying? Why are they buying? What brings customers to the door?"

These questions are still pertinent today and emphasize the importance of Marketing within any business. The better a business is at Marketing, the more profitable it will be. Of course that is true. But what is Marketing exactly?

Marketing is the function of business that **brings customers to your door,** and **culminates in some sort of sale.** The **Universal Business Model,** as introduced in Chapter Two, illustrates the importance of the marketing function as a part of the three big functions of business. The close correlation of **Marketing** (as shown in the following illustration) with the two other major business functions, **Production** and **Accounting,** leads to success.

UNIVERSAL BUSINESS MODEL
Phase III—When everything is working together

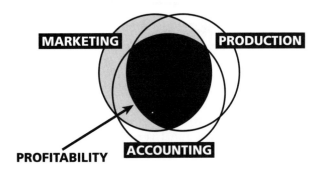

If you don't have a marketing plan, and a way to put it into effect, don't go into business! That seems logical. Doesn't everyone have a marketing plan? The reality is that thousands of businesses are started everyday by people who simply cross their fingers, hoping that customers find them, either randomly, or perhaps by Divine means.

Great customers do not just appear; they are made! Look at it this way: You have an amazing product that people are willing to pay for, and it has a great profit margin. Would you stop telling people about it? Marketing informs customers about your products, and brings them through the door. These three marketing principles can make your business more profitable.

Principle 1—Nothing happens until you make a sale!

This concept is critical to the success of any business operator or internal manager. What do you have to sell? How does that product or service meet your customers' needs? How do you get customers to your door so you can show them your product or service? If you do not have a method to sell, then there is no need to have a business. Everything **starts** with the sale.

Summarized below are the key concepts that support this important first principle.

◆ Every asset should be engaged in making sales. Everyone in the company must have a marketing mindset! Every employee should be involved in the sales process in some way. If he or she is not involved on the front line with customers themselves, then he or she should be supporting someone who is.

◆ Sales training is essential! Call a sales meeting often to see what is working, and what is not. Discuss changes in your sales techniques to enhance the skills of everyone. Include the office and production staff in these meetings, to hear their input, and remind them **that sales make the business flourish.**

The goal is to increase sales every day. The **Business Improvement Process** (discussed in Chapter Six) will outline the steps for improving the sales process.

♦ Every customer is a new customer. What works with one customer may not work with the next. Great sales people identify the needs and point of view of each new customer before they give the customers their own point of view. Then they meet the customers' needs with the products and services they are selling. These skills can be learned and transferred to others. That is the reason for sales meetings and training.

Everything you do in business is related to Marketing. Accounting should play an integral part of the marketing effort. How can an accounting system help in Marketing? Your accounting system should collect critical information for evaluation by the business operator. Your accounting system should provide the answers to the following questions which will support sales growth:

♦ What are customers buying? Where are they coming from? How much did each customer pay for the products and services you provide? How did they pay—cash or credit?

♦ What product lines are selling the most? What products have the greatest gross profit margin? How are these products selling, compared to other products? Which products are being returned? If financed, is there a correlation between the products sold on credit and bad debts?

♦ What is the cost of sales? Which assets are being used to create sales? (Remember, all assets in the business should be used in some way to promote sales.)

♦ What information from each sale needs to be collected to help in making future sales, and in responding to the customers' specific needs?

An associate of mine once took over the management of a car dealership that was really having some financial difficulty. In order to generate more cash, he sold one of the product lines to another company. It raised a lot of immediate cash. Then, after reviewing the accounting statements, he realized that this particular product line had been generating a large portion of the profit. Although he was able to solve a short-term cash problem, he created a longer-term problem. He then had to acquire other product lines to replace the moneymaker that was lost.

This problem could have been avoided altogether if the accounting system had been set up in order to give him the information that he needed to take immediate action. This accounting problem was soon remedied, but it took several months to re-build sales to previous levels.

Principle 2—A deal is only good when it is good for both parties.

Sales are critical to your business's success! But those sales must be good sales—meeting and exceeding customers' needs and proving profitable for you.

Recently, I was flying home from a meeting and I

wanted to rest and relax. I learned that the flight was undersold by quite a bit. I must admit, at first I was pleased by the thought of the extra space that I would have to spread out. But being a business owner, my thoughts quickly turned to the airline owners, recognizing that this flight might create a financial loss for them.

It occurred to me that, although it was a good deal for me, it may not be for the airline. If this situation persisted, the airline would eventually be forced to reduce flights or increase fares. Again, sales must be a good deal for both parties.

Sometimes sales go up and exceed your own expectations. Then you discover that you are not making the money you thought you would because expenses increased also. In some cases, I have discovered that expenses were even higher than sales, and were growing at a faster rate than sales. The owners did not even know it! They thought that if sales were increasing, they were almost automatically making more money. A better-designed accounting system helped them accurately manage this information.

Several years ago, my father recognized a demand for small, light-weight utility trailers that could be pulled by small cars, since they were beginning to take over the roads due to increasing gas prices. He had a trailer designed, then requested bids from local manufacturers. One manufacturer was significantly lower than the other two. He questioned the factory to make sure they hadn't made a mistake. They told him that the bid was correct.

As expected the 200 trailers sold quickly and he was ready to order 500 more. The manufacturer informed him that the price would have to double for the next group, because they had not included many of the costs in the original design.

So, my father had to go through the process of re-bidding the job, reworking the economics, and re-pricing the trailers. What appeared to be a good deal at first actually created more problems because the original deal was not good for both parties. The purpose of negotiating is to find a price point where the transaction is beneficial to the seller and the buyer.

Here are the key concepts that support Principle 2:

◆ WIIFM (*What's In It for Me?*) is a great way to remember this principle. If there is nothing in the deal that is good for me, why go through with it? And conversely, if there is nothing good in the deal for the customer, why should he or she go through with the transaction? The deal must be worthwhile for both sides.

Some sales may be good for the business, but not for the customer. You might benefit from short-term profits, but long-term customer relationships could be damaged. This can be true when you reduce quality without lowering prices, or when you knowingly take advantage of customers.

◆ Every customer has different needs. Ask for the customer's point of view. Then express your point of view, and decide how the sale will meet and exceed both parties' needs.

◆ Major customer motivators are health, wealth, and happiness. I have heard them expressed also as time, money and peace of mind. Whatever their motivation, show customers how your products provide benefits for that which they are searching.

One story I remember well was when an auto dealership sales manager, without permission, advertised an International Scout (an early type of Sports Utility Vehicle) at a ridiculously low price. When customers came in, the sales people would fill in the paperwork at the advertised price, and then ask: "Which transmission would you like?" The transmission was an option! The sales manager produced more traffic, but angered a lot of people. (This situation changed very quickly when the owner learned about the advertisement.)

Yes, sales need to be profitable. Customers' needs must be met also. And there must be a balance between the two. Don't ruin your most effective and least expensive marketing tool: "word of mouth" advertising. It can lead to your success or demise overnight.

Principle 3—Grow the business geometrically!

What does this really mean—growing your business geometrically? If you are not growing, you are dying! It is difficult, if not impossible, to remain the same year after year. Things change. The cost of financing changes quickly. The economy improves then worsens. Competitors come and go within the market. New technology and better products are developed and, all of a sudden, your products can become obsolete.

The business needs to grow to remain viable. And grow it will with the guidelines in this principle. Certainly, selling more of your existing products to existing customers makes sense, and plans need to be developed to do that. But linear growth is tedious and slows down over time.

Geometric growth comes from many different angles: from existing customers and from new customers, from existing products and from new products.

	EXISTING CUSTOMERS	**NEW CUSTOMERS**
Existing Services	Quadrant 1	Quadrant 2
New Services	Quadrant 3	Quadrant 4

Each quadrant indicates areas where your company can grow and is described below:

Selling existing products to existing customers.
(Quadrant 1)
- If you own a cherry orchard as a business, you would sell as many cherries as possible to the cus-

tomers you already have. Hopefully, this means that they would buy more than they are buying now.

Selling existing products to new customers.
(Quadrant 2)

♦ Following the cherry orchard example, the goal is to find new customers for the cherries you are growing. This may be through using different marketing strategies, different distribution channels, possibly even finding completely new markets, maybe overseas. The idea is to sell your cherries to new customers.

Selling new products to existing customers.
(Quadrant 3)

♦ Your cherry customers could have need for peaches, pears, apples and possibly many other complementary products to the ones you already sell—maybe even canned cherries, cherry juice, or pie tins. Ideally, these new products can be produced by you also. This provides additional sales through new angles.

Selling new products to new customers.
(Quadrant 4)

♦ This means that you could sell peaches, pears and apples to new customers, and then add cherries to what they are buying also.

This **geometric growth** is critical to the continued profitability of a business. **Keeping current customers** satisfied and loyal to you is important. A second angle is to **find more customers.** An additional

MARKETING   **33**

dimension is to persuade both current and future customers to spend more money with you more often. Still a third angle is to **develop new products.**

Let's examine these issues in more detail.

Keep your current customers:

Statistics show that it is much less costly to keep the customers you already have than it is to find new customers. (Source: Technical Assistance Research Project—1998). Once you have customers, you want to develop a loyalty in them so that they will never want to go elsewhere for the products and services they are buying from you right now.

A two-pronged plan is essential for dealing with existing customers. You must **keep them happy** with what they are buying from you already. Also, you want them to **spend more money** with you **and more often.** These are two critical objectives of a successful marketing plan for your business.

Customer service is imperative in keeping customers satisfied and loyal. It is a true differentiator in the market place.

Here are some guidelines:
Existing Customers/Existing Services
(Quadrant 1)
◆ Meet or exceed **agreed-upon customer expectations** 100% of the time. The key words are *agreed upon.* Customer expectations continually change so expectations need to be set early in the relationship so that, as a business, you can exceed them.

◆ Develop the concept of **customer loyalty** in all of your customers. This is done through constant communication with them about their needs, and how your products and services are meeting those needs. Customer loyalty is when a customer continues to buy from you, no matter what outside forces may try to pull away their business.

◆ Develop processes for dealing with customers consistently and promptly. Customers are fickle; one bad experience can erase many good experiences. Each transaction should be handled as if it is the very first transaction with that particular customer.

◆ Develop plans to have existing customers spend more money with your business. These questions can help with that analysis:

  – What else do they need that you can provide?

  – Is there any way that you can alter the arrangement to include some sort of regular monthly payment?

  – How can you increase residual sales or repeat sales?

  – Will they buy more of your existing products and services?

  – What new products and services are they searching for right now?

  – How can you motivate them to spend more money, more often?

– What types of complementary products and services could you offer existing customers that could help them meet their needs more effectively?

New Customers/Existing Services
(Quadrant 2)

I am never happy with my business unless it is growing. It is an imperative goal to grow, and to continually increase your customer base. Here are some questions that I have found helpful in analyzing how to find more customers:

◆ What new products and services do you need to develop to attract new customers?

◆ What kind of marketing research data do you have on which to make your Marketing and Product Development decisions?

◆ How can you customize your products and services for each new customer as they demand it?

◆ What easy offerings do you have for prospective customers?

◆ How can you improve prospective customers' awareness of your products and services without having to educate them exceedingly? (Education is much more time-consuming than Marketing; you want to stick with Marketing as much as possible.)

New Products/Existing and New Customers
(Quadrants 3 and 4)

The concept here is to develop new products that your existing customers and new customers can use. This is a critical part of the growth strategies for your business.

Here are some questions that can help in that analysis:

◆ What products are customers requesting, that you do not provide?

◆ Is it practical to develop these as new products?

◆ Is there new technology that could change the marketplace significantly in the near future; can you adapt this into your own product lines?

◆ What trends are you noticing in the marketplace that could affect what you will do in the near future?

Here is how a properly designed accounting system can help:

An up-to-date accounting system can provide vital information about your marketing efforts. The questions below could all be answered with a good accounting system. These are crucial in developing a pro-active marketing plan:

◆ What does an average customer spend with you during a typical customer's life?

- How often do you receive residual sales, or **complementary** sales, with little or no effort?

- What products and services are selling right now? Are they profitable?

- What products are being returned, and why?

- Are there some products that you should not be selling, because they are outdated, or they don't meet customers' needs anymore, or perhaps they are no longer profitable?

- What are the quality statistics about your products and services? (You could reduce the quality of the product or service, and initially be more profitable. But, in the longer term, this could hurt your reputation and your profitability.)

Revenue must exceed all expenses, including overhead. The only way to accurately know if this is occurring is if your accounting system is accurate and current. Data becomes information within the accounting system. This then becomes knowledge and wisdom for the decision makers trying to improve the marketing function in your business.

This process of increasing the effectiveness of your marketing efforts does not occur quickly. Chapter Six will outline a process for improvement that will make these principles come alive in your organization.

CHAPTER THREE REVIEW

Critical concepts to remember...

♦ Everyone in the company should have a marketing mindset.

♦ Nothing happens until you make a sale. If you do not have something to sell, do not go into business. The entire marketing effort culminates in a sale of some sort.

♦ A deal is only good if it is good for **both** parties. Negotiation is great between parties, but the final outcome has to be beneficial to both.

♦ Keep the customers you have, and find more. Your marketing efforts should be constantly focused on increasing revenue geometrically within the business.

♦ Your accounting system can provide you with valuable information about your sales process, **if it is kept current.**

Action Planning
CHAPTER THREE

Pertinent questions from this chapter:

- What are the profit margins on your current products and services? Are they still viable products and services in the marketplace? If you don't know, how can you find out?

_____

_____

- What information do you have available on which you base your marketing decisions?

_____

_____

- What does your four-quadrant marketing analysis show as growth opportunities in the near future?

	EXISTING CUSTOMERS	NEW CUSTOMERS
Existing Services	Quadrant 1	Quadrant 2
New Services	Quadrant 3	Quadrant 4

What are other significant learning points from this chapter?

_____

_____

ACTION ITEM	RESOURCES NEEDED	COMPLETION DATE

Notes...

Production

Become the Expert Inside your Business.

Employees are usually the greatest assets in any business. The relationships that are formed internally with each other, and externally with customers are critical to success. I have learned that when a business is in trouble, it is usually **not a "people"** problem, but rather a business **"systems" problem.** Correct the systems and the people become even more valuable.

When consulting, I ask these questions: "How are things going today? Where are the bottlenecks? What do we need to improve to make things run more effectively internally?" These questions focus on **Production,** or the internal workings of the business.

Production is a **profit center** for the business, with revenue and expense responsibility! If Marketing brings customers through the door, Production is what you do with them once they are there—from the time of the first sale through the entire relationship with the customer.

The **Universal Business Model** illustrates the importance of Production as one of the three big functions of any business. The close correlation of **Production** with the two other major business functions, **Marketing** and **Accounting,** leads to a more profitable and successful business.

UNIVERSAL BUSINESS MODEL
Phase III—When everything is working together

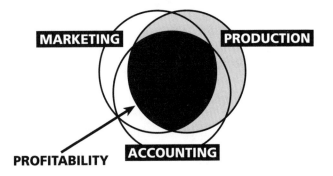

MARKETING   PRODUCTION

PROFITABILITY   ACCOUNTING

Production can be a revenue-generating activity. It may involve sales such as in retailing, and it begins when the customer first contacts the business. It can be very costly if expenses are out of control, perhaps even higher than the total revenue number. Internal production includes: sales closing, sales support, shipping, billing, manufacturing, scheduling and delivering services, developing new products and services, office support, quality control, etc.

People usually go into business because they are good at producing something; a new or improved product or service that is different or better than what already exists in the marketplace. Thus, of the three major functions in the **Universal Business Model,** Production is where you might feel the most comfortable.

Production can always be improved! Your business can be **more profitable** as you become a **Production Expert** inside your business. This chapter discusses the three **Production Principles** that can help improve the profitability of your business.

Principle 4— Pour on the Communication!

Communication can be likened to water in a garden. It provides the nourishment that allows employees to grow, and become more productive. By making sure the communication flow is getting to the "end of the row," it keeps everyone growing. It also promotes better understanding from the bottom to the top. Without regular communication, employees can feel unappreciated, and **Production** will suffer. **So, pour on the communication!**

Here are guidelines for successful communication within your business:

♦ **Sprinkle, Rain, or Flood.**

Communication with your employees has three levels: Sprinkle, Rain, and Flood. Each is effective when used properly.

Sprinkle (Casual)—This should occur as opportunity permits, having some contact with each employee on an unscheduled basis. This may be a brief conversation in the hall or in his or her office. Simply ask them how things are going. Let them know that you're available, and would like to help if they need anything.

Rain (Informal)—Regular newsletters or company activities are examples of this type of communication. Some newsletters go out weekly; others may occur monthly. In addition, some companies schedule Christmas luncheons and summer family activities.

At Universal Accounting Center, we use a weekly newsletter. Each week, progress of ongoing projects is discussed, and we announce future projects. We also use this opportunity to give credit where it is due.

This is also a good chance to remind each employee that the overall goal is to build the profitability of the company. We always address how each of them can be a "salesperson" in spreading the word about our products and services.

We also use this newsletter to recognize employee accomplishments. Recognition can take many different paths. It may be a pat on the back; it may be a fat paycheck, or it may be mentioned in the company newsletter. No matter how it occurs, it is usually appreciated and remembered. Some high tech firms use candy as a reward. This dates back to their start-up days when money was scarce. Still, the gesture indicates recognition.

Flood (Formal)—At least once per year, management should schedule a financial review with the employees describing the company's financial position, and plans for the future.

At Universal Accounting Center, in formal meetings, we discuss where we are going as a company over the next year, and over the next five years. We also discuss concerns, and seek their ideas on improvements.

- ◆ **Seek input from all of your employees.**

Involve employees in the setting of goals and solving of problems within the organization. **Ask for their input.** By doing this simple step, not only do you show your trust in them, but you are also facilitating their acceptance of the company's goals and progress.

Early in the dramatic growth of our company, we found a significant problem: we were running out of cash. Sales were higher than expected (a great problem to have), but nearly 90% of our sales were financed. Since the payments were split into monthly installments, our short-term cash was low, and we were forced to extend our own line of credit.

To address the problem, our management team met with our front-line sales people, and explained the problem to them. We told them that we needed to reduce financed sales to 65% or less of total sales to maintain an adequate cash position without having to go deeper into debt.

We were direct when we discussed the problem with them; then asked them to come up with a plan to solve the problem. I was amazed at their suggestions, many of which I had not even considered. A few of their suggestions would have hurt them financially if the situation did not improve.

We discussed their different recommendations, and decided as a group to implement those that we thought would meet the desired goals. Our total sales continued to grow, and financed sales fell to approximately 60%, better than our original goal. This achievement occurred because the employees involved in the situation came up with workable solutions that could be quickly implemented.

◆ **Share your plans with your employees.**

Most employees want to be a part of a growing, dynamic company. They want to feel that they are contributing in their own way. They want to know what is going on—whether it is through sprinkle, rain or flood tactics. What are facts vs. rumors? How is the business doing? Where is the business headed? How does each employee fit in?

Unless they feel management is open with them and will reward them for their contributions, they will not share their own ideas. You must set the example by being open about what is happening in your business, and what concerns you.

Financial information should be shared with the employees regularly—monthly, quarterly, and annually. Many times, employees do not know the expense of their desk, their chair, their office space, their phone, etc. Often, even this small amount of information can make a difference.

♦ **Give clear expectations.**

Having grown up in Utah, where the water is crystal clear as it cascades down the canyon streams, I was surprised to find that in most places in the U.S., naturally flowing water usually takes on a muddy look.

I find communication in most companies takes on a muddy look, and the employees have difficulty understanding what is expected of them. The key is to filter out all the day-to-day steps so that you can see the expected final result, and let the employees know specifically how their roles benefit the company. Then, let them assist in determining how to achieve the goal.

As with the muddy water, if you do not clearly describe your expectations, you are certain to get a different result than expected. Let them know the expected outcome, and also the boundaries in which you expect them to work. Keep them updated with the company's progress in areas that affect them.

Since communication is critical to the profitability of the business, try to improve it immediately. Start by asking questions, sharing information and listening to your employees and customers. This can lead to immediate results.

Principle 5—Improve Internal Processes.

As a business decision maker, you should always be searching for ways to better analyze and improve your organization's processes. This is best done by asking questions. In fact, you should never stop asking questions. "Is there a better way to do . . . ?" This is the basis of "continuous improvement"—always seeking a better way.

Every employee has either external customers (those who use your products and services and pay you money) or internal customers (those other employees for whom you provide service). Meeting the needs of all customers should be the primary focus of your employees. Customer needs are always changing; therefore, your processes need to be changing also. This is what **Quality** is all about—meeting and exceeding customer needs at the lowest possible cost.

Here are some guidelines for improving internal processes:

◆ **Find the problem—Create a solution—Get it done!**

Once you have identified the problem, or area for improvement, the first step is to brainstorm potential changes. Then, quantify the cost and potential revenues. Next, test your theory by making the changes. Finally, work for the results you want, evaluating all possible outcomes.

One client was receiving a higher number of returns from his Internet sales than from his storefront sales. In a survey of the customers who made the returns, it was found that customers who came into his store felt more satisfied than those who purchased from his web site.

They discussed the problem with their employees and decided to send a small "thank you" gift within two weeks of every purchase. That would give the customer a greater appreciation for the relationship, and consequently reduce returns. To test the theory, a gift was sent to every other customer that bought their product through the internet site. It was determined that returns were one third less common among those who received the gift, but still higher than the storefront sales.

So, the next test was to assign one sales person to call every customer who bought the product over the internet, and see if this would reduce returns even more. One question leads to another question, and so on. The goal was to solve a problem, meet customer needs, and reduce costs.

◆ **Use data and information from your accounting system to help solve problems.**

In the example above, you must understand two
critical numbers: What is the cost of a return, and
what will it cost to reduce returns. Certainly, if the
cost to reduce returns is more than the cost of
receiving the returns, then you may decide to take
no further action.

This information comes from your historical
database of revenues and expenses within your
accounting system. Without this information,
you're shooting in the dark, and missing most of
the time.

◆ **To solve problems and find the necessary
information, you need a complete accounting
system.**

The accounting system must be sufficiently
detailed to allow you to capture information in a
useful way.

One of the best ways to do this is to divide your
business into **profit centers,** and track your revenues and expenses accordingly. For instance, if you
have a restaurant that offers catering, you should
list these separately on your income statement as
two different businesses. Certainly, if your dining
room is losing money, but your catering business
is profitable, you may not want to extend your lease
when the time comes.

◆ **Continually benchmark against your competitors.**

One of the most insightful tools to identify your strengths and weaknesses is to compare your financial information with that of your competitors. To make this tool useful, you must analyze your business against other businesses in your industry of your equal size. This is called "Benchmarking."

From this study you can identify areas in which you're doing better, and want to maintain. More importantly, it will identify areas of interest where your competitors have figured out something you still need to learn.

Much competitive information is available for free, or for a nominal cost, from different business and industry associations across the country. (If you're not sure how to accomplish this, feel free to contact Universal Accounting Center and they can assist you in this process.)

Competition is a game of leapfrog, with your competitors seeing your improvements, meeting and even beating them. A company that settles back on its laurels will someday be surpassed by other companies which are continually improving.

Not all problems can be solved overnight. In fact, most can not. This principle can provide some intermediate steps that can be taken to improve processes in all areas of Production within the business.

Principle 6—Take what you have and make it better.

The focus here is developing a long-term approach to make things better within your business. As the world changes, you must change as well. One of the most published examples of this was when the inventor of quartz watches showed them to the largest Swiss watch makers. They sneered—said they would never catch on. Someone in Japan, on the other hand, recognized the value of never having to wind the watch, and began mass-producing them. Now watches made in Japan dominate the market.

The world is now the market place, even though you might not have a customer further away than 100 miles from your business. Rest assured that your competitors are looking at broadening their market base even if you are not. Becoming more efficient and effective is a constant process. Some projects will take months and maybe years to accomplish. Yet they are still worth it.

Here are some guidelines for taking what you have right now, and making it better in the long-term:

- ◆ **Ask critical strategic questions of your employees, customers, and economic forecasters:**
  - Where is the market heading?
  - What is happening in the world that could affect your business?
  - How can new technology make your business more profitable?

- How will each proposed project save or make money for the business?

- What types of synergy can you find in Production?

- How can you be better, faster, and cheaper all at once?

- How can you improve the quality of your products and services and meet customers' needs better?

◆ Hire people who are smarter than you!

Employees can make or break you, so hire the best and the smartest that you can afford. No person can be an expert in all areas of business. Partner with your employees to make things better, and then reward them for their efforts.

Sometimes the best manager is the one who knows the least about his or her particular industry. All too often, the manager is the best at his given field in the company, so he spends his time doing what the company does.

The problem is that he fails to **work on** his business and is happy to **work in** it. This means that all the company has is workers—nobody managing the business. Imagine a car with a gas pedal, brake, steering wheel, etc., but no driver. You get the picture.

Thus, a person who is not quite as familiar with

the day-to-day work could be more effective as a manager because he/she is spending time trying to determine how the entire business could be better run.

For instance, the president of most electrical construction companies is typically an electrician. So, what is he doing? He's out pulling wire, attaching outlets, and installing breaker boxes—things that he enjoys doing. Unfortunately, he's not managing the business, he's getting work done. What happens when this job is over? What about his finances? What about employment issues?

If the company was being led by someone that didn't know a 110-volt system from a 220 volt system (like me), I would be making sure that there was more work, and better work coming up, rather than being electrocuted.

♦ **Constantly check distribution channels for more effective, less costly ways of delivering products and services to customers.**

Delivery channels are constantly changing and becoming more efficient. Competitors may have lower prices and higher profits because of more effective distribution. Always be alert for better distribution methods..

♦ **Develop products that will sell without having to educate customers.**

Research and Development is part of the budget—

it keeps a company growing and vibrant. Your cost to market a product that already exists will be a fraction of the cost to sell a product that the public doesn't know they need yet. It's like selling ice cream in the middle of winter. Try coffee and warm cocoa instead.

Your best source for ideas could be your sales people. Ask them what their customers are asking for, and figure out a way to produce it.

These three principles are critical to the success of the **Production** function (the internal workings) of your business, and its overall profitability. A complete accounting system can provide much of the information needed to make sure these principles are effectively implemented. Maybe only two people are involved, maybe a dozen, or more. What is important is doing the **right thing, with the right people, in the right way, and at the right time.**

CHAPTER FOUR REVIEW

Critical concepts to remember...

- Pour on the communication! Employees are your most valuable asset, and constant communication with them is crucial to your success and profitability.

- Improve internal processes. All processes can and should be improved on a continual basis

- Take what you have and make it better. Some things can not be improved quickly. However, continual improvement should be a long-term objective of your business.

- If you can't improve, get out of the business!

Action Planning

CHAPTER FOUR

Pertinent questions from this chapter:

- Where are you, based on the *Wisdom Pyramid*, in each of your product and service areas? (data, information, knowledge, and wisdom)

  _____

  _____

- Looking at your internal processes, which do you think are satisfactory or better? Which have much need of improvement?

  _____

  _____

- What would your employees say are your expectations of them in general and more specifically, for this month?

  _____

  _____

- What are your exact costs for producing each of your products and services?

  _____

  _____

What are other significant learning points from this chapter?

_____

_____

ACTION ITEM	RESOURCES NEEDED	COMPLETION DATE

Notes...

Accounting

In The **Black,**
Profit is the Answer!

Over 500 years ago, Fra Luca Pacioli, the father of modern Accounting, said that three things were necessary for a successful business:

◆ Adequate cash.

◆ An adequate mathematician to work with the numbers.

◆ A system which can show at a glance the financial position of the business—in other words, an accounting system.

That wisdom remains true today. Yet, the **accounting** function is the **most neglected** of the three major functions in the **Universal Business Model.** The purpose of this chapter is to show you the importance of a good accounting system, and how the information derived from that system can be critical in improving the business.

Accounting is the function of business that gathers data and information from all the different aspects of the business. Business operators and managers can then use this information to develop knowledge and wisdom, and make better business decisions.

For several years, I worked for Exxon in Wyoming, as a Mine Accountant. I would spend every Friday in the mine, learning more about what was actually happening in the business, and how our costs reflected the action. For example, if I noticed that certain equipment was down or being repaired, then I would know that production quite possibly could be affected.

This hands-on experience was invaluable in understanding how the mine operated, and what exactly went into the accounting numbers. Because of this knowledge, I was able to provide better advice to the Mine Manager.

Years later, I visited a circuit board manufacturer who needed some help in controlling his cash. I asked for a tour of the facility to better understand the various processes that occurred within the plant. The Production Manager took me on the plant tour, and told me that this was the first time in over ten years that he had seen an Accountant on the plant floor.

My first recommendation to the Plant Manager was that the Accounting and the Production people needed to spend more time together! How can mutual understanding ever become effective without interaction between the two departments?

The **Universal Business Model** illustrates the importance of Accounting. As I indicated in Chapter Two, the closer the three major functions—**Marketing, Production, and Accounting**—work together, the more profitable the business can become.

UNIVERSAL BUSINESS MODEL
Phase III—When everything is working together

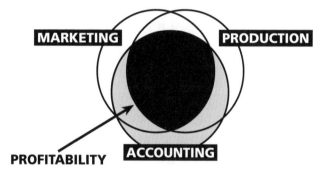

Every business needs a **Profit Expert.** That expert may or may not be in the Accounting Department, but the information he or she uses to analyze profit issues will definitely come from the accounting system. In many respects, your Business Accountant should be your best friend.

Over the years, I have run into countless small business owners who think that they are profitable, but who really don't know. The owner of a window washing company proved to be a typical example of this. He asked me how his business could become more successful. He had clients, and work was plentiful, but he wasn't making money. I asked him how he was utilizing the information he periodically received from his Accountant. He said that he only received information once a year in his tax return. BINGO!

He couldn't tell me how much money he was making in total, or his average revenue per client. He couldn't tell me what his costs were. So, with no Profit Expert in the business, there was no way of even knowing how to address the problems he had identified. Is it a surprise that **50% of businesses fail** within 6 months with this type of management?

For too many small businesses, Accounting is the function that business **owners** want to **ignore.** If not attended to, it becomes a weakness, and possibly could lead to the failure of the business. Just as you would never drive your car blindfolded, operating without accounting records means your financial vehicle is running without knowing where it is, where it has been, and where it is going. Sounds like a blindfold to me.

So, are there success stories out there? Absolutely, millions of them! There is probably not one company, with over 100 employees, that hasn't recognized the value of good records. They didn't become successful by mere coincidence. They know the value of information coming from the accounting system, and they are willing to invest the dollars necessary to make sure it is timely, accurate, and useful. Most have regular financial reviews with their management team to understand how their business is doing, and where it is heading.

I would watch my father in action when he visited the businesses that he managed. He would first visit with the sales people to see how sales were going. (That was really a check on Principle # 1—**Nothing happens until you make a sale.**) Then he would check with the other managers to see what problems and concerns had come up since his last visit, and what needed to be communicated to the employees. (That was a check on Principle #4—**Pour on the communication!**)

Next, he would visit with the Office Manager to check the important accounting indicators. I have **further developed and refined** these accounting indicators and principles while working with hundreds of businesses improving their profit picture.

SOME HELPFUL DEFINITIONS

The following definitions will help in the discussion of the principles dealing with the accounting function. (If you need further assistance with terms, please call your accountant or give us a call at Universal Accounting Center at 1-800-343-4827. You can also visit our glossary of accounting terms at www.areyouintheblack.com.)

The accounting system creates two important reports—**the Income Statement and the Balance Sheet.**

Income Statement—A summary of your performance over a period of time, usually a year. It is usually updated every month. The Income Statement shows the revenue coming in, the expenses associated with that revenue, and the profit or loss for that specific period of time.

Balance Sheet—A snapshot of your financial position at one specific point in time, usually updated every month. It is associated with the same ending date as the Income Statement.

Analyzing both reports is important in making profitable business decisions. (If you need further assistance or would like to examine sample Income Statements and Balance Sheets, please call your accountant or give us a call at Universal Accounting Center.)

Cash-based accounting system—An accounting system where sales are recorded when you receive the money, and expenses are incurred when you pay the bills. In its simplest form, the accounting system follows the cash, and it only records transactions when cash changes hands.

Accrual-based accounting system—An accounting system where sales are recorded when the sale occurs, no matter when you receive the cash. Expenses are incurred when you receive goods or services, even though you may not pay the bills for them until a later date.

An accrual type of accounting system more appropriately matches revenue with its associated expenses, irrespective of when the cash comes into or out of the business. This system can be complicated at first, both to implement, and to understand. But so are Marketing and Production until you gain experience.

Current Assets—A combination of cash and other assets, such as Accounts Receivable and Inventory, that can quickly be converted into cash.

Accounts Receivable—Amount of money owed to you by your customers.

Inventory—Stock on hand that is ready to sell to customers.

Accounts Payable—Amount of money that you owe to your suppliers.

Cash Flow—Amount of cash coming into your business and going out of your business during some time period—daily, weekly, or monthly.

Though accounting systems are inexpensive, they can become very costly in the hands of an untrained person. One of our clients had done his own accounting for the five years that he had been in business. Assuming that he was doing the accounting correctly, he would print out statements every month, and mail them out to his customers. He bragged that he had an excellent collection history with his customers.

However, at closer inspection we learned that his system had not posted many of his invoices because of the way that he was entering the sales. The unbilled invoices totaled $15,000 over the years; most of which he was never able to collect. So, how much had his accounting system cost him?

Here are the three accounting principles that are crucial in making sure your business operates profitably:

Principle #7—Cash flow! Cash flow! Cash flow!

Cash flow is the lifeblood of business. For new businesses, immediate cash is needed to create **future cash flow.** The first time the payroll is missed, you will know exactly how bad it is to be short of cash. How do you know how much cash you have in the business? Keep a check register. Call the bank! They can tell you very quickly. By the way, your accounting system should be able to match what the bank says. This needs to be the first place for improvement.

Here are some other observations about cash flow:

◆ In an accrual accounting system, you may have no cash, but show a big profit. You could be living in one world, and dreaming in another. Like most growing businesses, my company has experienced this. We permit our customers to pay us over 12 or 18 months. Our vendors won't wait that long for payment, and our employees don't want to miss their pay-days. The bank helps us by giving us a line of credit. When our cash needs are temporarily greater than what we have on hand, we use bank funds to take care of those cash needs. Then we pay the bank back when we receive the money from our customers.

♦ A business can have cash, but still be bankrupt. Enron had millions of dollars in the bank account when it was forced to shut down. You may have enough cash for this month, but not enough to make payments that are due in the upcoming months. Cash analysis is more than a current, monthly calculation.

♦ Cash is only one aspect of Current Assets. Current Assets are made up of cash in bank accounts, Accounts Receivable and Inventory. Cash could vary depending on what is happening with the other Current Assets. As Accounts Receivable or Inventory increase, then cash could decrease.

Current Liabilities are made up of current Accounts Payable, and the current part of long-term payables. Variations in Current Liabilities could also have a major bearing on how much cash is available, on any particular day. Thus, an analysis of cash must include an evaluation of all Current Asset and Current Liability accounts.

One of the strongest indicators of a company's financial stability is the **Current Ratio.** This is determined by dividing the total Current Liabilities into the total Current Assets. A ratio of 2 to 1 is desirable, meaning that the company should have twice as much in Current Assets than in Current Liabilities. Most businesses never attain that position. But then again, most businesses fail. (By the way, what's your Current Ratio?)

◆ Most often, a business may only need relatively modest sums of cash most of the time to run efficiently. Sometimes, there is more cash in the Cash Account than is needed to take care of upcoming payments. Cash should be earning interest, if it is not being used otherwise.

◆ Careful monitoring of cash is critical. An increase in your Accounts Receivable will usually decrease the amount of cash. Any purchase with cash could affect your Current Assets balance. Your cash on hand could change quickly as a result of changes in other assets.

With those observations made, here are some guidelines to help in your management of cash flow within your business:

◆ Even if your business is small, it is wise to establish separate accounts for business and home if you haven't yet. It is too easy to intermingle funds, and spend the cash for personal reasons, when it is needed to pay business debts. One client was confused because he had high profits but no cash (hint:

his wife was redecorating the house). Profitability does not reflect cash—this could be called the "High Profit—No Cash" syndrome.

◆ Manage your cash appropriately. You can have too much cash in the business. Cash is an asset that should be working at all times, gaining interest. Cash can be transferred among bank accounts, based on how much you need and when, and how much interest can be earned in the different accounts.

◆ Businesses should work within budgets—leaving some cash in the bank at all times. Work with your vendors so that your cash account does not fluctuate with highs and lows but is somewhat consistent through the year.

◆ Initially, every new business owner should expect to invest at least 50% of the necessary capital into their company. This lessens the amount of cash that will be needed from other costly sources.

◆ Leverage money effectively. When you start a new business, you will usually receive unfavorable terms from vendors. They want to be paid immediately, or in no later than thirty days. After establishing a good relationship with your vendors, ask them to extend your credit to 60 days, and eventually to 90 days.

It is amazing how negotiable they can become; they will not want to lose you as a reliable customer. Move from 30 days to 60 days to 90 days in paying your suppliers whenever possible. Use a credit card to extend cash flow for one more month. The benefit is to keep more cash in your own account for a longer period of time.

Watch the amount of recurring bills and expected receivables for the coming months. This will help you identify potential cash problems in the next couple of months.

Cash flow is crucial for every business as well as the proper management of that cash! Ask yourself how cash flow is handled within your organization.

Principle #8—Know Your Business.

Successful business operators and department managers know what is happening inside the business! You must have a sense of numbers and of understanding what they mean and how to influence them. If you do not have this sense of which numbers are important, then you need to hire someone that you can **trust** to look at the numbers and interpret them for you.

If you're not intimately aware of what is going on financially within your business, you may develop critical problems before you even know it. Long-term survival depends on your understanding of the company's financial condition. The answers to the following questions will help you better understand your business. They should be quickly and easily accessible from a well-tuned, accounting system.

- What are the daily, weekly, and monthly sales totals?

- What are the current cash totals available?

- What are accounts receivable and how old are they?

- What are the monthly payable numbers?

- Which products are selling?

- Where does the profit come from?

- Is our inventory current or obsolete?

- What are the major expenses for the business? How much are they?

- What are the overhead expenses?

- How does the business compare to last year at this time? Last month? Last quarter?

- What are the most important numbers you would like to see on a daily, weekly or monthly basis?

- What is working well in the business? What needs to be improved?

- How is our customer service working?

A **Professional Bookkeeper** and **Professional Tax Preparer** can be very beneficial to you as a business operator or department manager in helping you retrieve and analyze this information. These questions are not all-inclusive, but do provide a good start toward understanding what is really going on inside the business.

To be profitable and successful, these numbers need to be **the right numbers, done the right way, at the right time.** The answers to these questions will be found in the Income Statement or the Balance Sheet.

Several different types of analyses should be done on a monthly basis:

◆ "Score carding" is a term used to describe the important, even critical, numbers that a business owner or department manager can quickly scan to get a feeling for how the business is doing, and how it will be doing in the near future. These numbers are **key leading indicators** of the business, and, if they are in sync, the rest of the numbers that follow during the month should be okay.

Obviously, you **can not watch** everything all the time. Choose four or five numbers that are real indicators of how the business is doing, and watch them carefully. For example, most scorecards will have a quick summary from the following areas:

  – Marketing

  – Sales

  – Production

  – Customer Satisfaction

  – Cash Flow

Because each business is unique, leading indicator numbers can be different. The score card numbers I watch are **cash balance, current ratio, sales commission percentage, number of leads generated, and percentage of sales financed.** The major question for you is: What are the important numbers that you want to see daily and weekly in your business?

I recently helped a marketing manager create a "score card" for his group. We reviewed his processes, and determined that there were four productivity indicators that showed the results from his group. Until that time, he had always assumed that employee motion meant results.

Now, after spending some time quantifying the action, and observing the results, he has identified WHO and WHAT are driving his department's profitability. Furthermore, he discovered why a satellite office in another state has been struggling for the past year.

The "score card," illustrated below, quickly indicates important information about what is happening in this "example" business. The manager is interested in being able to monitor Marketing Leads Generated, Sales Closed, Production Completed, Customer Returns, and Cash On Hand. Based on this weekly or daily information, adjustments can be made quickly so that profit targets are maintained for the month, quarter and year.

Most of this information will come from the company's accounting system. This is only an example; your score card will probably look different.

EXAMPLE COMPANY SCORE CARD

DESCRIPTION	TARGET	WEEK 1	WEEK 2	WEEK 3	WEEK 4
MARKETING LEADS GENERATED					
SALES CLOSED					
PRODUCTION COMPLETED					
CUSTOMER RETURNS					
CASH ON HAND					

+ **Regular monitoring** is essential. Every time you make a decision, you should evaluate the impact that your decision will have on the Income Statement and the Balance Sheet.

Monitoring is also easier if your business is separated into distinguishable profit centers. Analysis of each profit center can let you know which areas of the business are doing well, and which need work. This analysis should be done on both a cash and accrual basis.

When evaluating your assets, you need to look beyond the tangible buildings and equipment. You should also list those items that don't show up on the Balance Sheet, such as your relationships, knowledge, location, and credit rating. Your job as a Business Manager is to maximize the value of every asset owned by the business.

Universal Accounting Center isn't worth much when considering the brick and mortar aspects, our asset of greatest value is our team of hard-working associates, the twenty-five years of successful graduates, and the relationships we have formed through the years.

◆ **Variance Analysis** is a process developed to understand the differences between expected and annual numbers, or trends between time periods. Analyze changes and trends at five levels:

– This month vs. last month

– This quarter vs. last quarter

– This quarter vs. same quarter last year

– YTD this year vs. YTD last year

– YTD vs. budget

Communicating the results of your analyses to all employees is helpful in making sure everyone knows where the business is going, and how well it is progressing. When employees know what you are measuring, it seems to improve. And if you cannot improve and be more profitable, sell the business.

Principle 9—Plan for Tomorrow

Business managers have a tendency to work so hard **IN** the business that they never work **ON** the business. **If you are not growing, you are dying!** Most business operators and department managers are so busy working in their respective jobs, involved in daily details, that they don't step back and look at the business or at the big picture. This Principle is a critical step in correcting that situation.

Michael Gerber (*The E-Myth*, HarperCollins Publishers, 1988) states that, as a general rule, CEO's should focus 90% of their time on the coming year and 10% on today. They should work on issues that will improve the business in some way.

The purpose of any planning process is to **improve profitability** in the longer term. Every business needs some sort of planning process—for the next day, the next week, the next month, and perhaps, most importantly, for the next year. Here are some important planning questions to ask about your next fiscal year:

◆ What are your major objectives for next year?

◆ Will you need new equipment? How much will that cost? When will you need it? How will you pay for it?

- Which profit centers are really working? Which are not? What changes need to be made?

- Will you need additional people? When? How many?

- What will the financial impact of the changes be, as you are planning for the future?

- How will these plans affect your profitability next year?

There are great benefits in having some sort of planning process. I would suggest that, because of constantly changing market conditions, it is probably not valuable to put great detail into planning for more than twelve months into the future. Here are some guidelines:

- A forecast gives you a **standard** to which you can compare actual results. Variations from your forecast can identify trends in the market place, departmental problems, dishonest employees, or faulty systems faster than anything else.

- A forecast forces you to look at the future—at least once a year—and to establish targets and objectives for business performance.

- A forecast puts everyone on the same roadmap traveling in the same direction.

- Forecasting should include a late-year discussion of the next 12 months. This discussion could include the use of the Business Improvement Process (discussed in Chapter Six.)

◆ Communication about business performance is most effective when all employees know the direction in which you are heading. The more the employees are involved in the planning process, the more effective the communication can be during the year.

◆ Planning gives you a chance to evaluate what the market value of your business is right now. Then you can determine what you want its value to be in three or five years.

SUMMARY

In the **Universal Business Model,** Accounting is as critical as Marketing and Production. The closer all three major functions of the business work together, the more profitable the business will be.

Accounting is more than just watching the balance in the checkbook. Every great business manager learned early the value of Accounting for the growth of their business. Minimally, you should plan to have one accountant for every 10 employees. If you have fewer than 10 employees, you should outsource the service to a **Professional Bookkeeper.**

For a list of Professional Bookkeepers in your area visit www.universalaccountingcenter.com.

These people, all certified by Universal Accounting Center and available in many areas throughout North America can provide the qualified analysis you need. Call Universal Accounting to find qualified people in your area.

Today's competitive market place demands more vigilance in watching your financial progress. This is not only true of knowing where you are right now, but you must also be conscious of where you have been, and where you are going. Then you must test, test, and test some more, to know what is working and what is not.

It is appropriate to note that, when seeking financing, a key indicator to a bank of your business strength is how well you demonstrate knowledge of your financial position regarding:

◆ The condition of your accounting system.

◆ Your awareness of your current financial position.

◆ Your plans for future growth.

CHAPTER FIVE REVIEW

Critical concepts to remember...

◆ The accounting function of a business is usually the most neglected of the three major functions in the Universal Business Model.

◆ Cash flow is the "life-blood" of any business.

◆ Understanding your business from an accounting perspective is critical in making successful and profitable decisions.

◆ Planning for growth is practically impossible without critical accounting information.

Action Planning

CHAPTER FIVE

Pertinent questions from this chapter:

- Where are you, based on the *Wisdom Pyramid*, in your understanding and implementation of your accounting system? (data, information, knowledge, wisdom)

_____

_____

- What are the key indicators that you should watch regularly, perhaps weekly or even daily, that let you know how well your company is doing right now?

_____

_____

- How would you rate the accuracy and completeness of your accounting system right now?

_____

_____

- What can you do right now to improve your accounting system?

_____

_____

What are other significant learning points from this chapter?

_____

_____

ACTION ITEM	RESOURCES NEEDED	COMPLETION DATE

Notes...

Putting it All Together

Based on my experience, I have developed an improvement process that works, especially in implementing the **Nine Principles.** This improvement process can ease the uncertainty that you may have felt when you studied these principles. It can help you develop specific plans for their implementation.

First, a **quick review** of critical concepts presented so far: The **Universal Business Model** (Chapter Two) illustrates the three major functions of business—**Marketing, Production, and Accounting**—working together. The center area, **IN THE BLACK**, represents profit and success—the bigger, the better. The accounting function is usually the weakest of the three, yet it is the one that brings the other two together better than anything else. This model forms the framework in which the **Nine Principles** work.

The UNIVERSAL BUSINESS MODEL—Phase III is illustrated below with Marketing, Production, and Accounting working closely together. This phase of the model maximizes the center core, or profit capability of the business, and illustrates how **IN THE BLACK** can work for you.

The **Nine Principles** (Chapters Three through Five) to make your business profitable fit within the **Universal Business Model,** with three principles in each of the three major functions.

The **Wisdom Pyramid** (Chapter Two) illustrates how knowledge and wisdom are gained. Data-based decisions are good; **wisdom-based decisions** are better! Business owners and internal department managers move up the Wisdom Pyramid by applying the **Nine Principles** and learning from each experience. An accurate and timely accounting system provides the data and information needed to gain knowledge and wisdom.

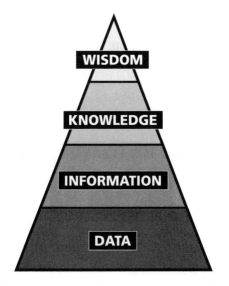

(Source is the work of W. Edwards Deming, and some of his quality work done after World War II. Other quality consultants have used similar models to illustrate how people learn.)

BUSINESS IMPROVEMENT PROCESS

If you cannot improve, get out of the business! That theme has been true in any business with which I have worked. Outlined below are the **Business Improvement Process steps (BIP's)** I use to implement the **Nine Principles.** These steps are not original; they have been around for some time. More importantly, they work! The real issue is making sure you develop action plans that will improve your business right now, rather than waiting for results to appear magically.

This improvement process can be used in all aspects of the business. The process can and should be used as a **cycle.** Once an action plan is completed, a new assessment can be started. It can be used daily, weekly, monthly, or whenever needed.

Perhaps another way to look at it is to say that you, as a business owner, department manager, or business accountant, should be in a constant state of analyzing the current situation in each of the three parts of the **Universal Business Model,** and implementing programs to improve. The following BIP's offer an excellent way to constantly improve your business functions.

The **Business Improvement Process** steps are summarized below:

1. Determine what the overall objectives are, and what you are evaluating. (This could include setting specific goals, both quantitative and qualitative, in the particular area you are analyzing.)

2. Determine what is working well right now, within the framework of the stated objectives.

3. Determine what is not working well. What are the problems behind what is not working well? What are the real causes? (Information defines the problem and can help determine causes. Solutions to the problems can be created when actual causes are identified.)

4. Develop specific action plans to improve on what is working well, and to correct what is not working well. At Universal Accounting Center, we use four words to describe what we want to accomplish in these plans:

Innovation, Quantification, Orchestration, and **Documentation.**

Innovation—What new way of doing things are we testing?

Quantification—How can this innovation be measured to see if it is really adding to the profitability of our business?

Orchestration—How will the actual implementation take place?

Documentation—How will the results be captured and stored? (This allows replication if it went well and adjustment if it didn't go well. Documentation adds to the collective body of knowledge or wisdom within the business).

(Source is Michael Gerber, *The E-Myth*, (New York: HarperCollins Publishers, 1988).

5. Implement action plans, assigning someone with accountability, responsibility, and access to necessary resources (the stewardship, if that is a better descriptive term) to complete the improvement process.

6. Start the Business Improvement Process over again. (There is always room to improve.)

As these **Business Improvement Process** steps are used, you gain more information, knowledge, and wisdom, which move you up the Wisdom Pyramid. This acquisition of information, knowledge, and wisdom leads to financial power—**truly intellectual**

property that you can use to make your business more profitable and successful overall.

The following worksheet puts the Business Improvement process in graphic form.

BUSINESS IMPROVEMENT PROCESS

1. Overall Objective	_____ _____ _____ _____
2. What is working well within the framework right now?	_____ _____ _____ _____
3. What is not working well right now?	_____ _____ _____ _____
4. Develop specific action plans to enhance what is working well and change what is not working well.	_____ _____ _____ _____
5. Implement action plans with accountability assigned, etc.	_____ _____ _____ _____
6. Start the process over again.	_____ _____ _____ _____

A DIFFERENT PERSPECTIVE ON THE NINE PRINCIPLES

The **Nine Principles** can be looked at from another perspective, one that you may not have realized previously. In each of the three groups of principles, one principle has **immediate** application, one principle has **intermediate** application and the third has **long-term** application. Let's re-examine the principles within this new framework:

Immediate Application:

1. Nothing happens until you make a sale.
   (From Marketing)

4. Pour on the communication!
   (From Production)

7. Cash Flow! Cash Flow! Cash Flow!
   (From Accounting)

Intermediate Application:

2. A deal is only good when it is good for both parties.
   (From Marketing)

5. Improve your internal processes.
   (From Production)

8. Know your business.
   (From Accounting)

Long-term Application:

3. Grow your business geometrically.
   (From Marketing)

6. Take what you have and make it better.
   (From Production)

9. Plan for tomorrow.
   (From Accounting)

Recently, I visited a farmers' market to buy produce. I was standing in front of a small stand, talking to a young sales person about his tomatoes. An older man, obviously the one in charge, came into the stand to re-supply the produce.

When I finished talking to the sales person, I was intrigued by the conversation between the two men. The first question the older man asked was: What have you sold while I was gone? The second question: How is the cash doing? And the third: What else do you need?

Very interesting, I thought, as I realized that the older man had just asked questions concerning all three of the **immediate application principles!** Those were the critical issues for him to know right then.

So it is with any business. When business owners go into their businesses, or business managers go into their departments, usually they want to know the very same information as the produce stand operator. Those are the questions of utmost importance on an **immediate** basis. Other questions concerning **intermediate** and **long-term** issues can be addressed later.

ACTION PLANNING

One concept that has helped me dramatically when working on action plans in the improvement process is the **APE** concept. The goal of any action plan should be **ACHIEVABLE, PROFITABLE, and EASY.** If any of the three are not fully in place, then the plan still needs some work before starting. This **APE** concept has helped on many occasions in keeping action plans from becoming too complicated.

For years, our training company had wrestled with the idea of creating a home-study, video-based, income tax preparation course. There were three perceived problems with such a venture, including price competition, simplifying the sophisticated tax laws, and keeping up with constantly changing tax rules.

The need, however, for this new product became more apparent each year as our accounting students repeatedly requested a comparable course for tax preparation. This demand caused us to call a meeting with representatives from our Marketing, Production, and Accounting departments. Their goal was to devise a method by which this course could be created in a way that made it **achievable** in a short time-frame (three months), **profitable** at a competitive price, and **easy** to update.

Thanks to their effort, the course was on the market within the desired time-frame allowed, and at a very competitive price, while producing a desirable income for the company.

So where do you start?

◆ Evaluate the immediate application principles by applying the Business Improvement Process steps to them.

◆ Create action plans for improvement in each area. These action plans should include attainable objectives, assignments for specific individuals, available resources, and time-tables for completion.

◆ The action plans should fall under the APE guidelines—Achievable, Profitable, and Easy.

The Business Improvement Process steps can help create action plans for each of the **immediate** application principles. How can sales be improved? How can communication be improved with employees and customers? How can cash flow be improved?

Doing this will address the most immediate improvements first. Once the **immediate** principles are addressed and applied, then follow the same process with the **intermediate** application principles, then with the **long-term** application principles.

ACCOUNTING AND THE BUSINESS IMPROVEMENT PROCESS

Wisdom is the key to being able to make good decisions. As we learn from the **Wisdom Pyramid** model, wisdom can only be gained through experience, and that comes from developing better information and knowledge on which to base our decisions.

Remember in Chapter One when I stated that after reading this book, I would like to hear readers say, **"Now I get it!** Now I understand why Accounting is so important in my business." Here's the reason why: Every one of the concepts mentioned in this action-planning section depends on information! Most of the necessary information comes from the accounting system. Good information will help ensure that action plans succeed, and business improvements are accomplished.

And after reading, it's not time to put down the book. It's time to get busy!

At Universal Accounting Center, we are constantly trying new ways of doing things. It could be a new sales method, a new internal process, or possibly a new way of looking at information which is captured in the accounting system. We have found, after much trial and error, that **these Business Improvement Process steps work.**

Each step is important. Not everything we have tried has worked. Yet, the accounting information we have gathered on each test was incredibly important in making further decisions about particular projects and tests. Clear measurement is critical, and documentation is essential, so that we can repeat our successes, and avoid making the same mistakes again.

Information becomes intellectual **property—or wisdom—in the Wisdom Pyramid** model. One of my early clients owned a gas station on a busy corner of our town. He had the gas pumps, car repair bays, and a small office where he could process the money and credit cards. He watched as more and more gas stations retrofitted their stations to include a convenience store. He resisted and resisted as his gas business declined lower and lower. In fact, he never did make the switch except for a cooler with pop and milk. His station, once thriving, is now closed.

SUMMARY

Growing your business is not an option—it is a responsibility. Too many people depend upon you, whether it be your family, or your employees and their families. If you are not growing, eventually your competition will push you out of the market. If I ever hear a business owner say: "I am satisfied with the way my business is right now," I know I have found one more business that will probably be gone in five years.

The goal of working so hard to implement these principles is to become more profitable and successful. The secondary goal is to make the three functions in the **Universal Business Model** work more closely together.

The **benefits** of using these principles are enormous:

◆ Your business will be more profitable. That is the number one benefit.

◆ You will have a sound understanding of your financial position, and a clear monitoring system of your cash flow needs.

- You will have a quantified expectation of future results.

- You can gain wisdom more quickly now that you realize how it is developed.

- People will work together more effectively when they understand what you are trying to accomplish.

- You will be dealing with problems which will be fun problems. How do you handle so much growth? How can you develop even more synergy in the business? (I have found that business life is much more enjoyable when I am dealing with **good problems.**)

I could probably make this a very long list. Accounting information is so important to the profitability and success of your business.

As I mentioned in the Foreword, you (like me) may never be able to play golf like Arnold Palmer. But you can learn and develop skills that can help your business and your career. These **Nine Principles** have helped me manage my businesses. **And more importantly, they can help you by bringing you more profits and great success!**

Here they are for review one more time:

NINE PRINCIPLES TO MAKE YOUR BUSINESS PROFITABLE

1. Nothing happens until you make a sale!

2. A deal is only good when it is good for both parties.

3. Grow your business geometrically.

4. Pour on the communication.

5. Improve your internal processes.

6. Take what you have and make it better.

7. Cash flow! Cash flow! Cash flow!

8. Know your business.

9. Plan for tomorrow.

CHAPTER SIX REVIEW

Critical concepts to remember...

◆ The Business Improvement Process illustrates a **proven process** for improving all aspects of your business starting right now.

◆ The **Nine Principles** can be examined from a **time perspective**—three principles can be applied **immediately,** three principles can be applied in the **near** future, and three principles are designed to be implemented over the **long-term.**

◆ Action plans should be **Achievable, Profitable, and Easy (APE).**

◆ Accounting information and training are the key elements in business improvement.

Action Planning

CHAPTER SIX

Pertinent questions from this chapter:

- How could you improve your sales and marketing processes by using the 6-step Business Improvement Process?

  _____

  _____

- How could you improve your internal business processes by using the 6-step Business Improvement Process?

  _____

  _____

- How could you improve your accounting processes by using the 6-step Business Improvement Process?

  _____

  _____

- How could you use the A (Achievable), P (Profitable), and E (Easy) concept in your business planning?

  _____

  _____

What are other significant learning points from this chapter?

_____

_____

ACTION ITEM	RESOURCES NEEDED	COMPLETION DATE
Read *Red to Black in 30 Days* when it comes out.		

Notes...

_____

_____

_____

_____

_____

_____

_____

_____

_____

_____

_____

_____

_____

_____

_____

_____

_____

_____

_____

_____

_____

_____

**Turn the page to learn about what's new at
Universal Accounting Center!**

UNIVERSAL ACCOUNTING CENTER
5288 South Commerce Drive
Salt Lake City, Utah 84107

Dear Reader,

Thank you for taking the time to read **in the BLACK, Nine Principles to Make Your Business Profitable.** I enjoyed writing it, and I hope you found it helpful in your own pursuit of higher profitability and success.

I had four objectives for writing this book...

◆ To promote the **Nine Principles** to make your business more profitable. They will work for you!

◆ To introduce you to the Universal Business Model with the Wisdom Pyramid. These models can help you dramatically in the managing process.

◆ To enhance the role of Accounting within your business. Rather than being a necessary evil that creates a burden for business, Accounting is truly the language of business that defines profit.

◆ To help accountants and bookkeepers realize how important their services are within business organizations.

Consider using this book as a topic of discussion for the next six weeks, reviewing each chapter with your team and applying these principles in your business. Start today on the path toward launching your business into a more successful and lucrative future!

Great resources are available to help your business become more profitable. UAC consultants can offer assistance in training you and your staff to ensure that implementation of these **Nine Principles** is as effective as possible.

Call us now at 800.343.4827 and talk to one of our business consultants. The call is free and UAC can help you start now in making your business more profitable. You can also check our web site at www.areyouintheblack.com.

Again, thanks for reading **in the BLACK.**

Allen B. Bostrom CPA

P.S. Enjoy a preview of my newest book,
Red to Black in 30 Days.

RED TO BLACK IN 30 DAYS
By Allen B. Bostrom, CPA

Turn the page for a preview of

RED TO BLACK IN 30 DAYS

A business turnaround primer
for small business accountants

FOREWORD

This book shows you how to grow your accounting practice, make more money and gain expertise in helping troubled small businesses—making them profitable once and for all. It is a guide to *quick* small business turnarounds.

You know small business owners; they have a never-ending supply of problems. Some problems are serious and some are not, but they are always there. The problems are rarely anticipated and sometimes, these business owners cannot see the problems right before their very eyes.

Then, all of a sudden, there is not enough cash to last through the end of the month or even through the end of the week! Or maybe expenses are out-of-control. Or sales drop unexpectedly. Desperation sets in quickly.

Where do these small business owners turn for help?

Usually their accountants gets the first visit—if they have one. If *you* are the accountant, you may be the only person in a position to help turn the business around and become profitable! You can be the business owner's *Profit Expert*—or turnaround expert.

As a Profit Expert, you can advise the business owner as to what he can do right now to make the business more profitable. This book can be your coach if you do not currently have that expertise!

The book is divided into three parts: **DISCOVER, DEVELOP,** and **DOCUMENT.** The three parts follow a continuous improvement model that can be applied to all aspects of the business.

PART I—DISCOVER—sets the stage for how small business accountants can help in business turnaround situations—turnarounds that need to be made right now, not in six months or even 90 days.

Even 60 days may seem like an eternity. Some actions need to be taken immediately. The next 30 days are critical!

Our tendency is to rush too quickly into action. You want to *do* something the first day that will help the business recover. However, before you do anything, you need to discover what is going on in your own practice and in your business relationship with the business owner. The turnaround project needs to be set up correctly so that you and the business owner can each reach your goals. Then you can proceed to the **DEVELOP** phase.

PART II—DEVELOP—outlines the six action steps in the turnaround process. The book provides the models, processes, and monitoring tools necessary for developing and implementing a turnaround plan.

The six action steps work. The process starts with an assessment that will enable you to formulate a plan to navigate those activities that are easiest to control within the business. The process progresses through marketing and building revenue. Reassessment is done at the end of this section to see what progress has been made and what still needs to be done. When this work is done, one major phase remains:

PART III—DOCUMENT—captures the major learning points from the turnaround process for the business owner specifically regarding his own business. Then the accountant can focus on what he learned that can help in the growth of his own accounting practice.

You don't *have* to follow this process; you can try something else if you want. But this process works!

Is this the answer to every problem?

Probably not! Not all small businesses can be turned around, and not all of them in 30 days. But if a business can be turned around, the process and tools presented in this book will help!

Read on. You'll find plenty of answers here.

PART I - DISCOVER
WHAT IS GOING ON HERE?

INTRODUCTION
Making a Difference

Your accounting practice is steady or growing slowly. You want it to grow more quickly, with more and better clients, more revenue and more challenging projects. Some of your small business clients have big problems and you may feel uncomfortable or inadequate to help them. You need a coach yourself or a guidebook you can use to help you deal with small business clients that are in trouble. This is your guide book!

YOU CAN MAKE A DIFFERENCE

As the accountant you may be the first one to see and understand that the business is either having trouble or headed for trouble. The information from the financial statements can be life-saving when communicated to business owners in a timely fashion. You have the responsibility to tell business owners there are major problems if you know about them.

This communication can be a real wake-up call to the business owner. But there is hope! You can help; you want to be associated with these businesses for a long time and want it around for a long time.

The models and the processes outlined in this book will become second nature to you. This expertise will allow you to expand or even specialize your accounting practice in business turnarounds. If you are an internal accountant, this book provides strategies and tactics that can make you much more valuable within your organization.

YOU CAN MAKE MORE MONEY

Of course, you need to be compensated for your work. That itself might be your biggest problem. How do you collect payment if the businesses you work for are struggling? This book will help you with that as well.

Instead of charging clients for monthly or quarterly compilations of accounting information, you can charge them for your work as a trusted advisor and turnaround consultant.

Perhaps most importantly, the processes and models outlined in this book enable you to expand your accounting practice and make more money. Expertise in business turnaround strategies will increase the value of your services, and you can charge your clients accordingly.

You can prove your value as an accountant and the value of accounting information. You can gain a reputation as a profit and growth expert. And perhaps, for compensation, you can take earn a small monthly commission and a percentage of future profits. If the business is currently losing money, the business owner will experience little or no risk in giving you a percentage of future profits. He will be better off than he is right now, and so will you.

MY OBJECTIVE FOR WRITING THIS BOOK

Here are two reasons why I wrote this book:

First, accounting students, clients, small business owners and small business accountants ask me many questions. The question I hear the most is:

How can I help a small business owner turn around his business quickly—like right now, not in months, but in a matter of days or weeks? This book addresses that question by outlining a process that will work for any small business.

The second reason I wrote this book is because the first book I wrote *(In the BLACK—Nine Principles to Make Your Business Profitable)* focused on how to *make* and *keep* your business profitable. It did not address ways for turning a business around—making a profitable business out of one that might be headed for closure in perhaps a matter of days or weeks. This book answers that question: *How can a business be turned around quickly?* This book fills that crucial need.

A quick review of *In the BLACK—Nine Principles to Make Your Business Profitable* is appropriate here to set the stage for subsequent chapters. Here is a quick summary of the nine principles from my first book:

The first three principles are for marketing; the second three for production; the last three for accounting—the three major functions of any small business.

1. Nothing happens until you make a sale!
2. A deal is only good when it is good for both parties.
3. Grow your business geometrically.

4. Pour on the communication.
5. Improve your internal processes.
6. Take what you have and make it better

7. Cash flow! Cash flow! Cash flow!
8. Know your business.
9. Plan for tomorrow.

There is another way of looking at the nine principles. Three are short-term in nature, three are medium-term, and three are long-term. Short-term principles are those that need to be addressed today. They can have an immediate effect on company results.

SHORT-TERM PRINCIPLES:
1. Nothing happens until you make a sale!
4. Pour on the communication.
7. Cash flow! Cash flow! Cash flow!

Medium-term principles are those that need to be addressed but won't have an instant effect on the business like the short-term principles do. They are very important, however, and need to be addressed.

MEDIUM-TERM PRINCIPLES:
2. A deal is only good when it is good for both parties.
5. Improve your internal processes.
8. Know your business.

Long-term principles focus on critical issues that need to be addressed in any company over an extended period. But they will not change the results of the business overnight.

LONG-TERM PRINCIPLES:
3. Grow your business geometrically.
6. Take what you have and make it better.
9. Plan for tomorrow.

In the Black contains great material for small business owners looking to take a systems approach to their business processes to ensure they are profitable. *Red to Black in 30 Days,* however, is much more of a how-to book, helping you to answer the very valuable question: how do you turn troubled small businesses around quickly so they can be profitable.

YOUR OBJECTIVE FOR READING THE BOOK

Now you know why I wrote the book. Here are a few ideas why you should read the book:

- It can help you develop your skills in helping troubled small businesses become profitable.

- It can help you become more proficient in these skills if you already have worked with troubled small businesses.

- It can help you master the models and processes necessary to make you a *Profit Expert*.

Many skills are involved in becoming proficient in turnaround strategies and tactics, and they are all outlined in this book. Included are project management skills with practical guidelines to help you set up projects correctly. The book discusses the work that needs to be done and how to complete it. It also covers setting up a timeframe in which you will complete that work and how you will be compensated for it.

The working relationship between the accountant and the business owner needs to be thought through carefully so that each understands his roles and responsibilities. Accounting information and additional business management expertise are both valuable when advising a business owner through a turnaround situation. You can truly become a Profit Expert.

As a Profit Expert, you can gain the business owner's respect with a focused analysis of the problems facing the business and your sound recommendations and workable solutions in resolving them. You will be valued *from the start*—a factor that will make you successful and secure your new position as Profit Expert. Your reputation as a turnaround specialist will spread and you will find new clients. Or, I should say, your reputation will help clients find you.

You have an additional goal. You want to procure a one-year management and accounting agreement with the business owner as part of the turnaround process. This shows the business owner that you know what you are doing and believe in the business as well as your process for saving it—it can survive this 30-day crisis and be a viable, healthy business one year from now and beyond.

You want to be associated with healthy, profitable, and growing companies. Your accounting and business management expertise can change your relationship with the business owner—all for the better.

BOOK ORGANIZATION

The book has nine chapters divided into three parts.

The **DISCOVER** phase includes Chapters One and Two. Chapter One focuses on becoming a Profit Expert. Chapter Two focuses on setting up the turnaround project correctly.

The **DEVELOP** phase covers the six action steps in the turnaround process with one chapter devoted to each step.

Chapter Three outlines Step 1: Assessing the Situation. Chapter Four describes Step 2 where you develop a succinct, practical turnaround plan based on the assessment results. You and the business owner should agree to use this plan as a guide during the turnaround project.

Chapters Five, Six, and Seven focus on action steps: controlling cash, reducing expenses and increasing revenue. You need to have control of certain systems—accounting, cash management, expense authorization—during the turnaround process. This planning document will assign roles and responsibilities.

Chapter Eight focuses on monitoring and reassessing the business situation, seeing what happened during the 30-day turnaround period. In some cases, these steps will be enough to stabilize the business, and that is our number one goal. In other cases, these 30 days represents the first iteration in the stabilization and growth process.

The **DOCUMENT** phase is described in Chapter Nine.

Chapter Nine allows you to document the major points that you and the business owner learned about his particular business. You have both assessed improvements that have been made in the business during the 30 days and what still needs to be accomplished. Your task here is to document the business management expertise gained by both you and the business owner as you have worked to make the business be more successful.

Chapter Nine also allows you do document what you learned in enhancing your Profit Expert skills. These learning points should be written down and documented so you do not have to learn those things again.

This knowledge becomes business wisdom! This wisdom increases your expertise as an accountant, business manager, relationship builder and most importantly, as a Profit Expert. This wisdom includes what you have learned that will help you in your next turnaround project. Don't skip this step.

Frequently Asked Questions

Who should read this book?

Accountants and small business advisors, whether they are external or internal, who work with small businesses and want to be more effective should read this book. The concepts in the book will make you a *better advisor, a Profit Expert*—to the small business owner.

A small business, for the purpose of this book, is any privately-held business with 20 employees or less. Decisions can be made quickly, overnight, maybe by one person, without input from outsiders. One week in these small businesses or even one day might see drastic changes in cash, prices, processes, procedures and people.

WHAT IS THIS THIRTY DAYS ALL ABOUT?
(The time it takes to go from Red to Black)

In this book, the thirty days is broken into 6 five-day work weeks. The timing—it could take 30 weeks or 30 hours—is not as important as the concepts and steps.

Of course some turnaround projects may take longer than 6 weeks. This book will outline a process that needs to be followed in turning small business problems around, irrespective of the time needed for the project. The emphasis, however, in this book will be on what can be accomplished in 30 days.

WHAT ARE REALISTIC EXPECTATIONS FOR 30 DAYS?

To show a profit! To do this, the small business must be able to adjust quickly to proposed changes. The process is important and sometimes 30 days is just not long enough.

Because these businesses have less than 20 employees, they can make quick adjustments—some within days and maybe hours to help implement turnaround strategies. This is a critical concept.

HOW SHOULD YOU READ THIS BOOK?

Sequentially at first, then as a reference manual. It is a process-driven, project-driven book that will be helpful in turning an accountant into a turnaround expert. Important process models are provided for you to follow in helping small businesses turn around.

The book provides a logical progression from assessment through execution of the plan to stabilize small businesses that are in trouble. It will follow the turnaround process and progress through three case studies. These cases are introduced at the end of this chapter.

The book stays above the detail that some accountants love to see and analyze. That is intentional. In the following chapters, I address strategy, tactics and tools and how they can be used. This book will not get lost in detail.

I realize that many small business accountants and many small business owners are female. But for the sake of clarity and succinctness, this book will be using masculine pronouns and adjectives. Please take no offense. It simplifies the text.

SUMMARY—WHERE YOU SHOULD BE AT THIS POINT

Many books have been written for the small business owner. This book focuses on the small business accountant. The models, systems and processes outlined in this book will help you consult any small business but particularly those that are struggling.

You need to decide right now if this is the type of work you want to do in your accounting practice. You can make a difference in these troubled small businesses. Your skills as a Profit Expert and business manager are critical now!

As a business manager and advisor, you can outline a process to follow for stabilization of the business and help the small business owner make decisions that can lead to increased profitability. Effective communication of that information and your recommendations are critical in establishing and enhancing the relationship with the business owner.

Key Learning Points

- You can make a difference in unprofitable small businesses. You can become a turnaround expert by using the strategies, tactics, tools and models presented in this book. This book can be your coach and guide through the process.

- Your roles as accountant, business manager, and Profit Expert are critical in small business turnaround situations. You can be a Profit Expert by providing advice that can help the business owner make better, more effective decisions. You can make more money in your accounting practice with a variety of compensation methods.

- *In the BLACK* concepts form the foundation for the turnaround concepts in this book.

- Turnarounds can occur in 30 days or less in many cases—and you can be a catalyst to those changes. This is especially true in organizations where there are less than 20 employees.

Not all small businesses will turnaround in 30 days. Some have inherent problems that cannot be solved quickly, and maybe not at all. But if the small business can be turned around, the concepts in this book will help. This book will focus on what can be done in 30 days.

CASE STUDY INTRODUCTION

Subsequent chapters will follow three small businesses as they attempt to quickly turn around from unprofitable and other adverse situations. Each small business has unique problems but a Profit Expert can help in all cases.

Here is the background information on each:

CASE I
Miriam's Art and Frame Shop

Miriam's Art and Frame Shop has been in business since 1995. It provides wholesale framing to designers and has 5 employees. This is a sole proprietorship and her financial statements show a healthy profit. But she never seems to have any cash in the bank. Miriam hasn't taken a paycheck for the last three months.

You are Miriam's accountant and her sister-in-law. You are quite competent but she doesn't use your services for more much than quarterly financial statements and tax work. It is difficult to schedule Miriam's time to discuss business problems because she is always busy. You don't press the issue too much because it is hard to talk to a relative about financial problems.

You know, however, there are serious cash problems in the business! And you will need to force a meeting with Miriam in the near future to make her aware of what the accounting information says about her business. You have some recommendations for Miriam if she will only listen.

You are willing to become more involved in the business to ensure its success because you think the business has real potential. Miriam doesn't have much cash to pay you right now but you could agree to a small monthly fee and a percentage of future profits. She may agree to your help because she's definitely needs it.

CASE II
Knecht Roofing and Construction

Knecht Roofing does roofing for several general contractors and any interested private parties. He has been in business since 2000. Kevin *seems* to be successful and is always busy. He brags about getting almost every bid he submits.

He should be rich. He has plenty of backlog but shows very low profit on his income statements. His wife does the bookkeeping for him but she needs help putting together monthly and quarterly financial statements.

Customers seem to be happy with his work and he has great references. He needs two more roofers but doesn't know where the money will come from to pay them.

You are the outside accountant who generates quarterly tax and financial statements for Knecht. You will get the first call when Roger realizes something is terribly wrong and his wife doesn't know the answers.

How will you get paid for your services? You don't want to be a partial owner of the company because working with Kevin on a constant basis would be very difficult. Cash or a percentage of the profits or revenue might be the only way to go in this situation.

But you do need a new roof yourself. Maybe that is the way to get compensated.

CASE III
Sherwood's SureSave Market and Auto Repair

Sherwood's SureSave Market and Auto Repair has been on the same corner for over 25 years. Until recently it had *cornered* the market for the area, being the only convenience store, gas station and auto repair shop for almost a mile. It is a great location at that.

Tom, the owner, and his son, perform all the maintenance in the three auto bays located behind the store which remain busy all the time. They have three employees who run the convenience store and the front-end business. The gasoline pumps are old as is all of the front-end equipment.

Last year, a grocery store with discounted gas pumps opened on the opposite corner. Sales in the convenience store and at the pumps have been declining ever since the new store opened. Profits have dropped significantly and before long, the business itself might fail!

You are the outside accountant that Tom calls when he needs business advice. You know the business is currently experiencing many problems with more on the way. You have considered providing direction to Tom and his son.

They can afford your going accounting rate on a monthly basis. This may stretch your skills, however, because they need more help marketing than they do with internal operations.

These case studies will be updated at the end of each chapter to see what improvements can be made using **Red to Black** principles. Which of these businesses will survive? What will they look like at the end of the thirty-day turnaround period?

Pick up Allen's new book now from Universal Accounting Center!

UniversalAccountingCenter.com

Notes…

Notes…

Notes…

Notes…

Notes...

ABOUT THE AUTHOR

Allen B. Bostrom, CPA

Allen is the President of Universal Accounting Center based in Salt Lake City, Utah. He has over 30 years working with businesses of all sizes and has taught over 30,000 people different aspects of Accounting and Business Management.

He is a much sought-after speaker and presenter promoting the importance of using accounting information in business decision making and other small business management strategies and tactics. He is the author of a new book: *Red to Black in 30 Days* and many accounting and business management articles.

The mission of Universal Accounting Center is to provide accounting-based products and services that maximize organizational profitability and individual effectiveness. *In the Black—Nine Principles to Make Your Business Profitable* and *Red to Black in 30 Days* complement both those initiatives.

Allen lives in Sandy, Utah, with his wife Sheri and their four children.